The Lessons of Maria Woodworth-Etter on *Miracles*

LARRY KEEFAUVER,
GENERAL EDITOR

CREATION
HOUSE
Orlando, FL

THE LESSONS OF MARIA WOODWORTH-ETTER ON MIRACLES
A Charisma Classics Bible Study
Larry Keefauver, General Editor
Published by Creation House
Strang Communications Company
600 Rinehart Road
Lake Mary, Florida 32746
Web site: http://www.creationhouse.com

Unless otherwise noted, all Scripture quotations are from the
King James Version of the Bible.

Contents

Introduction

WELCOME TO this devotional study guide on *The Lessons of Maria Woodworth-Etter on Miracles*. This study is a companion volume to *The Original Maria Woodworth-Etter Devotional*.

This devotional study is part of a series of four Bible study guides focused on the teachings of some of the founding leaders of the Spirit-filled and Pentecostal movements—Smith Wigglesworth, John G. Lake, Maria Woodworth-Etter, and William J. Seymour from Azusa Street. Do not feel that you must go through this series in any particular order. Choose the guides and sequence that best meet your spiritual needs.

Let's turn for a moment to meet Maria Woodworth-Etter, a remarkable woman of faith. In a day when Pentecostalism was derided and women in ministry were scorned, Maria Woodworth-Etter blazed a passionate trail across America. She held powerful evangelistic meetings where thousands were saved and healed. Enduring the sharp criticisms of mainline religious leaders, she fearlessly listened to God's voice and helped to pioneer Pentecostalism in the early 1900s.

Born July 22, 1844, in Ohio, to parents who were not Christians, Maria did attend a Christian (Disciples) church. Her father died an alcoholic, leaving Maria's mother in poverty with eight children to raise. At the age of thirteen, Maria went forward in her Disciples church to accept Christ. She was not saved, however, until the next day when, at her baptism, God's power so overwhelmed her that she fainted in the Spirit. She heard

Jesus call her into ministry, but her church did not use women in ministry at that time in any Christian vocation except as missionaries.

She married Mr. Woodworth, and they prepared to become missionaries. She suffered poverty, the death of children, and the onset of her own poor health. Maria Woodworth-Etter saw these trials as preparations for ministry. She became involved with Friends (Quakers), and for a time worshiped with them. She and her husband continued to work hard and save money for a trip west, which would be her missionary outreach. She preached wherever a church would let her and raised offerings for mission work.

After twenty-six stormy years of marriage, P. H. Woodworth's infidelity was revealed and, in January 1891, they were divorced. On the first day of January 1902, she married S. P. Etter. Together they continued her evangelistic ministry.

As she spoke one evening to a packed meeting of Disciples, the baptism of the Holy Spirit came over her. She wrote, "It seemed as if the house were full of the glory of God. I felt as if I were drawn up over the people." She preached in a place called "The Devil's Den," and revival broke out. She continued to preach revivals and started two churches. Her fiery preaching was accompanied by miracles, healings, visions, prophesies, tongues, and deliverances through the early 1900s.

These devotional studies contain her words taken from her sermons and from diary records that document her meetings through 1916. Maria Woodworth-Etter was a Spirit-baptized contemporary of William Seymour, Charles Parham, Smith Wigglesworth, John G. Lake, and the Pentecostal outpouring that accompanied Azusa Street in 1906 and the subsequent years. A forerunner of

Kathryn Kuhlman, Maria Woodworth-Etter was used mightily of God to demonstrate that the power of the Holy Spirit is as real in these days as in the church of Acts.

This devotional study guide may be used by individuals, groups, or classes. A leader's guide for group or class sessions is provided at the end of this devotional study for those using this guide in a group setting. Groups using this guide should complete their devotional studies prior to their group sessions. This will greatly enhance sharing, studying, and praying together.

Individuals going through this guide can use it for daily devotional reading and study. The purpose of this guide is to help the reader(s) understand miracles throughout the Scriptures with the insights of Maria Woodworth-Etter. All of the insights quoted from Etter's precise words are placed between lines and italicized for easy recognition. Each daily devotional study is structured to:

- ❖ Probe deeply into the Scriptures.
- ❖ Examine one's own personal relationship with Jesus Christ.
- ❖ Discover biblical truths about miracles.
- ❖ Encounter the person of Jesus Christ as personal Lord and Savior.

It is our prayer that as you study about miracles daily in this devotional study, your life will be empowered by the Holy Spirit to trust Jesus Christ in every aspect of your life and to minister in His power and miracles as He promised, "He that believeth on me, the works that I do shall he do also; and greater works than these shall he do, because I go unto my Father" (John 14:12).

Day 1

God's Power

But as many as received him, to them gave he power to become the sons of God, even to them that believe on his name.

—JOHN 1:12

JESUS HAS ALL *power. He was raised up with all power. The Holy Ghost was with the disciples, but Jesus said, "He shall be in you."*

When they were all together, Jesus met with them, and He opened their spiritual minds. "He breathed on them, and saith unto them, Receive ye the Holy Ghost" (John 20:22). They received Him, and became partakers of the divine nature. They received the gift of God, were enlightened, and cried out, "My Lord and my God." No one ever had that experience before that time. They were sons of God by the new birth. "Yea, for the rebellious also." Eternal life is the most important of all gifts. For without this gift you can never get inside the pearly gates.

There is no power apart from a personal relationship with Jesus Christ. We repent, are obedient in baptism, and receive the gift of the Holy Spirit (Acts 2:38). In the Spirit is all power to live eternally and to live a life filled with signs and wonders. Read the following scriptures, and write down the power available to you as a child of God through faith in Christ:

Acts 1:8

Romans 15:13

2 Corinthians 12:9

Ephesians 1:18–21; 3:20

Philippians 3:10

Colossians 1:10–11

HEN THE SINNER *stops his rebellion and repents, God gives him faith to accept Christ. God gives him power to become a son of God, born, not of man or of the will of men, or of flesh and blood, but by the power of God. He is then no longer a rebel, but a son, for he has received the gift of God and has been born of the spiritual family of God. His name has been written in the family record by the finger of God, and it has been said, "This man was born in Zion." He has the finished work on Calvary for sin and uncleanness. He is now a child of God, ready for any or all of the gifts of the Pentecostal baptism and power. He is God's man.*

What blocks the power of God in your life? As God's child, His miracle-working power (*dunamis*) is available to you at all times and in all situations. But hindrances can arise to block that power and thus impede miracles in your life. Check any of the hindrances listed below that may presently be blocking God's power in your life:

❏ Unconfessed sin
❏ Pride
❏ Rebellion
❏ Unbelief
❏ Disobedience
❏ Other: _____

Ask Yourself . . .

❖ Do you have a personal relationship by faith with Jesus Christ?
❖ Is the Spirit's power flowing freely and without hindrance in your life?

If Jesus is not your personal Lord and Savior, pray: *Jesus Christ, I trust You as my Lord and Savior. I repent of my sins and confess that You are the Son of God. I ask You to forgive my sins through Your shed blood. I receive the gift of Your Holy Spirit. Thank You for saving me. Amen.*

If you are a born-again child of God, pray: *Fill me, Lord Jesus, with Your Holy Spirit. Flow through me with Your miracle-working power. Amen.*

Day 2

Signs and Wonders

*And by the hands of the apostles were many signs and
wonders wrought among the people.*

—ACTS 5:12

WHEN THE DISCIPLES *were put into prison, their lives threatened
on account of God's great power within them for healing and
miracles, they were forbidden to preach in the name of Jesus.*

*Those early Christians knew it was the power of God that caused
all their persecution. They knew if they had a form of religion, and
denied the power, that they would have no more trouble. But, beloved,
they said, "We will be true to God. We will preach the Word if we die."
Then they prayed to the Lord, saying, "Lord, behold their threaten-
ings: and grant unto thy servants, that with all boldness they may
speak thy word, by stretching forth thine hand to heal; and that signs
and wonders may be done by the name of thy holy child Jesus" (Acts
4:29–30).*

*When they preached they knew they must see the signs of the pres-
ence of the invisible Christ, who confirms His Word through their
message in their meetings. Then, like Peter, they could say to those
present, "This that you see and hear and feel, it is the promise of the
Father, it is the Holy Ghost" (Acts 2:33, author's paraphrase).*

*The Son was pleased with their prayer and with their faith and
courage. The place was shaken, "And they were all filled with the Holy
Ghost and they spake the word of God with boldness" (Acts 4:31).*

The life of the early church was filled with the presence of the Holy Spirit who performed signs and wonders in their midst. Survey the first five chapters of the Book of Acts. List below ten evidences of the power of the Holy Spirit that were manifested in the early church. Circle the manisfestations evident in your church today:

1. _____

2. _____

3. _____

4. _____

5. _____

6. _____

7. _____

8. _____

9. _____

10. _____

A FTER THIS EVENT *they had greater success. God did mighty signs and wonders at the hands of the apostles. Great fear fell on all the church, and on all that heard and saw these things. Multitudes of men and women came flocking to Christ.*

The greatest miracle witnessed in the early church was salvation. Salvation resulted as the gospel was preached in boldness, and the fear of God brought repentance to the lost. Before miracles are manifested, the fear of God and repentance must be present in the church. Read the following scriptures, and write down what they say to you about repentance.

Matthew 4:17 _____

_____

Acts 2:38 _____

_____

Acts 3:19 _____

_____

2 Corinthians 7:10 _____

_____

Ask Yourself . . .

❖ Do you fear the Lord? Has repentance turned your life totally toward Him?
❖ What miracles are being manifested in your life?

Write a prayer repenting of any sin in your life and asking God to manifest His power and miracles in and through you:

_____

_____

_____

Day 3

A Form of Godliness

Having a form of godliness, but denying the power thereof: from such turn away.

—2 TIMOTHY 3:5

THOSE WHO ARE *opposing the demonstration of the Spirit today say we do not need these things, that we are progressing with the age, that we want an intellectual religion, and that we must explain and present the Word from a human standpoint in a scientific way.*

Are you experiencing the miracle-working power of God in your life and church? If not, then *a form of godliness* or of human religion and tradition may be hindering the power of God. Human reason cannot decipher and understand God's miracles. Read 1 Corinthians 1:18–2:16, and then complete the following sentences:

Human wisdom cannot _____

_____ .

The ways in which God's wisdom is manifested are _____

_____ .

Spiritual things are understood by _____ .

Believers have _____

_____ .

I N THESE LAST *days the masses of so-called religious teachers belong to the class Paul described—those who have a form of godliness but deny the power (2 Tim. 3:5). From such, we must turn away. They will not endure sound doctrine and will turn the people away from the truth.*

These false teachers are in a worse condition than the Jews. They are sinning against much greater light. They are willingly blind and are teaching their followers to hide behind a refuge of lies, trusting the doctrines and traditions of men. "In vain they do worship me," saith the Lord (Matt. 15:9). The judgments of God are coming upon the false church in the most awful way.

Human ways and traditions stifle the power of the Holy Spirit. Paul writes, "Quench not the Spirit" (1 Thess. 5:19). Remove from your life anything unholy or rooted in a form of godliness that quenches the Spirit's power (2 Cor. 7:1). Read 1 Thessalonians 4:1–12, and then write a prayer repenting of anything in your life that would quench the Spirit:

_____

_____

_____

Ask Yourself . . .

❖ What forms of godliness tempt you to deny the power of God?

❖ How is the Holy Spirit sanctifying you daily?

Almighty God, I repent of sin. Purify and sanctify me that I might be a vessel of honor for You. Amen.

Day 4

Holy Spirit Power

But ye shall receive power, after that the Holy Ghost
is come upon you.

—ACTS 1:8

EARNEST INTEREST ON *the part of the workers was not by any*
means confined to the Stone Church people or those most
intimately connected with the work. It was not a Stone Church
affair but catholic in its broadness.

All who came, even from a distance, threw themselves into the
work of praying with the sick with much earnestness, showing in a
marked way the growing spirit of unity. There was no building up of
"My work," which naturally characterizes individual effort, but on
every hand it was evidenced that all were unselfishly working in the
interest of Christ's body. Missions and churches were forgotten in the
united effort to get souls to God.

God honored the faith of all, and people who had their eyes on
Him received healing regardless of who prayed for them. One sick
woman who came in mistook one of the sisters for Sister Etter, and
asked for her prayers. The sick woman was immediately healed. We
hope this will be an encouragement to some sufferers to whom Mrs.
Etter cannot minister. Healing flowed all through the church at
different hours; not only in the meetings but during the day. Here and
there you would see groups of people praying for the sick, and shouts
of glory from the suffering ones told that the lightning from heaven
had touched their bodies.

When God's power flows through His vessels of honor, then signs and wonders are manifested in the body of Christ. What signs and wonders are you observing in your church? For what are you praying? Check below all that applies to you and your church.

MIRACLES IN THE CHURCH

We are seeing . . .   **We need to see . . .**

❏	Physical healing miracles	❏
❏	Inner healing of emotions	❏
❏	Financial miracles	❏
❏	Salvations	❏
❏	Deliverances	❏
❏	Miracles of revival	❏
❏	Miracles of restoration	❏
❏	Other:_____	❏

---

*T*HE REVIVAL, WHICH *lasted for six months and was at its flood through July, was not due to any distinctions in theology or to the setting forth of any particular doctrine or creed, but because we have been getting back to the simplicity of the gospel, and with much prayer.*

Miracles happen when the gospel is presented with simplicity and boldness in the atmosphere of prayer.

Read Acts 2:41–47. In your own words describe how the early church lived and moved in the power of God:

_____

_____

_____

Day 4

Ask Yourself . . .

❖ How is my church and life like that of the early church? Not like the early church?

❖ What needs to happen in my life so that His miracles and power are manifested?

Write a prayer asking God to empower your life and church with what the early church had of Christ's power and miracles:

_____

_____

_____

Day 5

The Fire Falls

And I, if I be lifted up from the earth, will draw all men unto me.

—JOHN 12:32

FOR TWO YEARS *Brother Foster and the saints had been calling me to Topeka to hold a convention. At last we felt that the Lord was leading, so the last week of July 1915, I, with several good workers, landed in the beautiful city of Topeka.*

Many of my readers have read of the great meeting we had in that city twenty-seven years ago, when I went with two young girls and a janitor as strangers, at the invitation of one minister, and held meetings for nearly two months in the beautiful park.

The dear Lord Jesus says, "If I be lifted up, I shall draw all men unto Me."

Miracles never point to us—only to Jesus. Miracles happen when He receives glory. Read Acts 8:4–25, and answer the following questions:

What did Simon want? _____

_____

How did he propose to get what he wanted? _____

_____

How did Peter respond? _____

_____

Do you want the Holy Spirit's power in your life? _____

_____

What must you do? _____

_____

    Miracles are not available at our beck and call. Christ sovereignly works His miracles as He chooses. We cannot buy, manipulate, or control His power for our own purposes. He alone will receive glory for what He does.

    What miracles have you seen in your life? Write a prayer giving Christ glory for those miracles:

_____

_____

_____

E IS THE great drawing power. As we preached the Word, giving Him the preeminence above all men and powers, the Lord was with us, confirming the Word with signs and wonders.

*   They began to bring the sick on beds and crutches, the lame, the blind, and the halt were seen running from their cots and beds. The blind were made to see, the lame were leaping and shouting. Sinners wept their way to Calvary, and arose praising the Lord for they had found Him precious to their souls. Many times the places of amusement were empty, the great theater was crowded, and many could not get in. Many ministers of different faiths came from all parts on trains, in companies, bringing the sick with them.*

Are you witnessing such revival? Are other groups of Christians working in harmony with your church to reach the lost in your community? Is Jesus being lifted up and drawing all men to Himself where you live? How are you praising and giving glory to God for what He has done in your life? Circle everything that you are doing to give Him glory:

Praying   Praising
Worshiping   Witnessing
Giving   Loving God and others
Ministering to the least of these
Lifting up Jesus at home and work
Other: _____

Ask Yourself . . .

❖ How will I lift up Jesus today?
❖ What am I doing to avoid taking any glory away from Jesus?

Write a prayer giving Jesus all the glory for what He is doing right now in your life:

_____

_____

_____

Day 6

Speaking in Tongues

And they were all filled with the Holy Ghost, and began to speak with other tongues, as the Spirit gave them utterance.

—ACTS 2:4

THE HOLY GHOST *is a wonderful person, not a myth or shadow. Pentecost, when the Holy Ghost came in to stay, is the greatest thing that ever happened in God's work. He came and took possession of one hundred twenty men and women; He sat upon their heads in cloven tongues of fire. He took possession of their bodies; then of their vocal organs; and they spoke, everyone, as He gave them utterance.*

They spoke in languages they had never learned, and did not know what they were saying. The Holy Ghost took possession of their tongues, and spoke through them; He spoke through the clay as you would speak through a telephone and told about Jesus. "He shall testify of Me."

Has the Holy Spirit taken over your tongue? Is every word coming out of your mouth that He would have you say, or are your words those which come out of your own thoughts and flesh?

Describe how the Holy Spirit speaks through your tongue: _____

_____

ESUS TOLD THE *apostles that they should be witnesses. When the Holy Ghost came, He knew all about it, and through the apostles He told of the wonderful works of God. When this was noised abroad, multitudes gathered. It was the speaking in tongues that drew the people. When the people heard the apostles, they were confounded and said, "What meaneth this?"*

I want you to notice this point — it was speaking in tongues that confounded them. The Holy Ghost spoke through these unlearned men who had never been to college to learn other languages. It was one of the most wonderful things God ever did. It is now, when God speaks through you.

God speaks through totally surrendered vessels. The Holy Spirit desires to speak through you just as He spoke through those early disciples. When they were baptized by the Spirit, they spoke boldly in His power. That was a miracle. Before Pentecost, the disciples were in hiding. After the Spirit's baptism at Pentecost they were proclaiming Christ boldly on the streets.

Read Romans 1:16–17. Paraphrase it, and rewrite it in your own words:

_____

_____

_____

Day 6

Ask Yourself . . .

- ❖ How is God speaking through me? When am I boldly witnessing?
- ❖ Have I totally surrendered my tongue to the Spirit?

Write a prayer asking the Holy Spirit to baptize you and speak through you:

_____

_____

_____

Day 7

A Sign to Unbelievers

Wherefore tongues are for a sign, not to them that believe, but to them that believe not.

—1 CORINTHIANS 14:22

OD SENDS THE *Holy Ghost to come into the human body. He takes charge of the vocal organs, and the person has nothing to do about it. But, for all that God does—such wonderful things—some of you will not believe it. Tongues are for a sign to unbelievers. In Acts, they were the worst kind of unbelievers—they had crucified the Lord. Nonetheless, they were made to believe in Jesus Christ by this sign. They were convinced by this sign that Jesus was the Messiah, when everything else had failed.*

In Acts 2, tongues were a sign for the unbelievers of the miracle-working power of God. They witnessed God's Spirit speaking through Spirit-baptized disciples. The baptism of God's Spirit and the confirming sign of tongues appear elsewhere in Acts. Read the following scriptures, and write down how the Holy Spirit confirms His power through tongues:

Acts 10 _____

_____

Day 7

Acts 19:1–7 _____

_____

Mark 16:15–18 _____

_____

HESE WERE UNLEARNED *men, all Galileans, yet they spoke all the tongues representing the different nations in a wonderful way. It takes years and years to master other languages, and very few speak other languages fluently like natives. These were unlearned people, yet they spoke fluently, like the natives, because God Almighty spoke through them.*

Everyone who is baptized in the Holy Ghost today, as he ought to be, speaks in another language, and the first words almost always are, "Jesus is coming soon!"

What is the Holy Spirit saying through you? How have you encountered the baptism of the Spirit? His baptism brings cleansing fire (Matt. 3:11–12; Luke 3:16–17) and power (Acts 1:8). Describe the baptism of the Holy Spirit in your life:

_____

_____

_____

Ask Yourself . . .

❖   Are you experiencing all the power that the Holy Spirit has for you through His baptism?

❖   What evidences of power from the Spirit are you witnessing in your life?

Write a prayer asking Jesus to baptize you with the Holy Spirit and fire:

_____

_____

_____

Day 8

Greater Works

*Verily, verily, I say unto you, He that believeth on me,
the works that I do shall he do also; and greater works
than these shall he do; because I go unto my Father.*
—JOHN 14:12

JESUS HAS LEFT *His work in our hands. It means something
wonderful to be baptized in the Holy Ghost. The Jews were
unbelieving until they heard the Holy Ghost speaking in other
tongues through those unlearned people. They knew it was God. They
realized they had crucified the Lord, that He had risen and gone to
glory, and they cried out, "What shall we do?"*

*Jesus prayed on the cross, "Father, forgive them, for they know not
what they do." When the Holy Ghost came they knew what they had
done. The tongues were a sign to unbelievers. Today it is one of the
greatest things God ever did.*

How do you respond when you witness the sign of
tongues? Check any of the responses that you have:

❏ Awe and wonder
❏ The hunger to hear God
❏ Fear of God
❏ Confusion and bewilderment
❏ Uncomfortable
❏ Excited
❏ Joyful
❏ Distracted

❏ Judgmental of those speaking in tongues
❏ Other: _____

Read Acts 2, and describe the different ways people responded to the disciples speaking in tongues:

_____

_____

_____

---

*T*HE HOLY GHOST *will sing through us: He is training us to sing at the marriage supper of the Lamb. We shall not all die, but we shall all be changed. We shall have a glorious body, like Jesus, and shall rise to meet Him in the air, full of joy.*

People who are healed are full of joy and sometimes jump and dance when the healing power comes into them. The Holy Ghost takes all the deadness and stiffness out of them; sometimes God slays them and lays them down so He can talk to them.

Men and women, rejoice, seek the baptism, and receive the gifts. You shall have them if you believe for them; and you shall be witnesses. May God seal this in your heart, in the name of Jesus.

With the baptism of the Holy Spirit come both power and joy. Read the following passages about the great joy present in the believer's life, and write down what Scripture reveals about that joy:

Matthew 5:11–12 _____

_____

Luke 10:20–21

John 16:16–33

Romans 5:1–2

Philippians 4:4–7

1 Peter 1:1–9

Ask Yourself . . .

❖ How are you experiencing His joy in your life?
❖ How are you sharing your joy in the Lord with others?

Write a prayer asking Jesus to fill you with joy in the Holy Spirit:

Day 9

Former and Latter Rain

Behold, the husbandman waiteth for the precious fruit of the earth, and hath long patience for it, until he receive the early and latter rain.

—James 5:7

I N THE EAST *they had the early rain to start the grain. They could not tell anything about the harvest until they received the latter rain. If it came abundantly there would be a good harvest.*

The apostle says to us, "Wait for the latter rain; be ye also patient unto the coming of the Lord." When the latter rain is falling we know the coming of the Lord is near. We are getting the early rain, and will get the latter rain before long. He is getting the bride ready.

The apostle is speaking to the church. If any one is sick among you, don't run for the doctor or send him to the hospital, but let the sick ones send for the elders. The elders were supposed to be men endued with the Holy Ghost, who would come and pray over him, anointing him with oil, and he should be raised up. If he had sinned in any way, he must confess it, and through prayer, be forgiven.

Have you ever had the elders pray for your healing? If so, describe what happened? If not, explain when you would go to the elders for prayer: _____

_____

_____

OME PEOPLE SAY *this is spiritual healing. They are blind because they want to be. Anointing with oil is a symbol of the anointing with the Holy Ghost. A barrel of oil would not heal. But if you are anointing with faith and obedience, you will get the blessing.*

It is the healing virtue of Jesus and the power of God. After the disease is cast out, the healing power of Jesus comes in. The prayer of faith shall save the sick. The power of God cleanses the soul, and the sick one is raised up, both soul and body.

In Scripture, oil represents the Holy Spirit. He alone heals and sets us free. He cleanses us through the blood of Christ. Read this entire passage—James 5:7–18. Make a list of all the needs in your life that you would like to ask the elders to pray with you about:

1. _____   5. _____
2. _____   6. _____
3. _____   7. _____
4. _____   8. _____

Ask Yourself . . .

❖ When will you ask the Holy Spirit to heal you physically and emotionally?

❖ When will you ask the elders to anoint you with oil and pray with you?

Write a prayer of faith for the sick persons that you know, asking God to heal them:

_____

_____

_____

Day 10

Pray With the Sick

And the prayer of faith shall save the sick, and the Lord shall raise him up; and if he have committed sins, they shall be forgiven.

—JAMES 5:15

ANY OF GOD'S *children, filled with the Holy Ghost, can pray with the sick, anointing with oil in the name of the Lord. You can rely upon it: the person will be raised up.*

You can pray for and anoint the sick without any special gift. Pray for one another. People may die before help can reach them. Call in the neighbors, and unite in prayer. If there has been any backbiting confess it.

Have you ever prayed for the sick? Has anyone that you have prayed for been healed? When you pray for the sick, what attitudes do you have as you pray? Circle all that apply:

Faith   Hope   Expectation
Doubt   Uncertainty   Fear
Love   Joy   Assurance
Other: _____

HE PRAYER OF *faith is effectual, and availeth much. If you cannot get anyone with a special gift, pray for each other. I know many people who have not had a doctor in the family. Parents pray for the children, and children pray for the parents. Little folk who can hardly talk will pray, and the sick are raised up.*

Pray one for another. Wherever you are, Jesus is. He is the healer and also the baptizer. He gives the resurrection life. Many today are wonderfully healed while alone with God. God is moving in a marvelous way. We must exercise faith and obedience.

Praying for others is not an option, it is a command. Throughout the Word we are commanded to pray for others. Read these scriptures, and write down what they say about praying:

2 Chronicles 7:14 _____

_____

Matthew 6 _____

_____

Ephesians 6:18 _____

_____

1 Thessalonians 5:17 _____

_____

Philippians 4:16 _____

_____

Day 10

Ask Yourself . . .

❖ Are you praying for others in faith and obedience?

❖ For whom do you need to pray right now?

Write a list of needs that others have, and then pray for individuals by name and need.

_____

_____

_____

Day 11

Laying on Hands

They shall lay hands on the sick, and they shall recover.
—MARK 16:18

I WAS HOLDING A *meeting in Indiana; there were few people there to pray the power down. Dr. Daggett, a physician, came to the meetings whenever he could and would lead in prayer.*

Sometimes he had to go out, he suffered so with pain in his knees. The Lord began to say to me, "That man ought to be healed." He impressed this upon me so much, I had to go to him and say, "I wish you did not have to go out; I need you here." He said, "I am very sorry, but I suffer so I have to go." I asked him if he did not believe God could heal him, and told him that I believed God wanted to heal him.

God was working with him in the same way. So I called the congregation together and said, "Are there any Christians here who believe God can heal? If you really believe, come and help me. I am going to pray for healing."

Several came. I did not know what to do any more than a baby. I began to pray; the power of the Lord raised my right arm up until it was over Dr. Daggett's knee and then stopped, for I did not like to touch it. The power of God was in my hand, and He wanted me to lay my hand on that man's knee.

When I understood what God wanted, I laid my hand on the knee and asked God to take the disease out. Dr. Daggett sprang to his feet, healed. He had been in discomfort for twelve years; everyone knew him, and everyone was amazed.

Miracles happen when by faith in Jesus believers lay hands on others and pray. The power of the Holy Spirit is communicated through the touch of one who prays in faith. Read the following scriptures and then, beside the praying hands below, write down what happens when we pray by faith and lay hands on the sick (Matt. 8:3, 15; Mark 6:56, 8:23–25, 16:18; Acts 8:17, 9:12, 13:3, 19:6, 28:8):

When I lay hands on the sick and pray for them, I feel . . . (put an *x* where you are):

Confident   Frightened

Filled with the Spirit   Empty

Bold in faith   Doubtful

Excited   Cautious

As you pray by faith for the sick, you will witness the miracle-working power of God. Be bold, and reach out. Touch the sick, and pray for their healing.

Ask Yourself . . .

- ❖ Do I usually pray first or medicate first?
- ❖ Do I really believe that God heals?

Write a prayer asking God for boldness in laying hands on and praying for the sick:

_____

_____

_____

Day 12

The Power of God

That your faith should not stand in the wisdom of men, but in the power of God.

—1 CORINTHIANS 2:5

HERE ARE MANY *powers in the world that are not of God, but are counterfeit. But where there is a counterfeit power, there is always a genuine power. No one ever tries to counterfeit anything that is not genuine—a sure evidence that it is genuine.*

The devil shows his power in a good many ways to deceive people. He tries to substitute some other power for the power of God. It was so in the time of Moses and in the time of the prophets. God's power was in the world—especially so at certain times. Then magicians would come up with their powers and show something that seemed similar. One power was God and the other power was the devil.

How do we know if the spiritual power being manifested is truly from God, or counterfeit? First John teaches us how to test the spirits. Read 1 John 4:1–10, and complete the following sentences:

The Spirit of God confesses _____

_____.

Other spirits not from God do not _____

_____.

Greater is _____

_____ .

Love is manifested when _____

_____ .

OSES WENT TO *Egypt to lead the people out. He threw down his rod before Pharaoh, and it became a living serpent. The magicians said they had the same power, so they threw some rods down, and their rods became serpents. Moses did not get scared and run away. He knew the power of God, and he wouldn't have run if all the serpents in Egypt had come before him.*

He stood his ground, and I admire him for it. I do not like a coward. What was the result? Moses' serpent swallowed the others up, heads and tails! There was nothing left of them. Those who are trying to overthrow the power of God and substitute something else will have a day of judgment. The time is coming when the almighty power of God will swallow them up, the day of His wrath.

Why do some people oppose the Spirit of God working miracles today? Check all the reasons you have observed for their opposition:

❏ Fear
❏ Unbelief
❏ Rebellion
❏ Anger at God
❏ Lack of understanding
❏ Intellectual reasoning against miracles
❏ Hurts because God did not respond to past needs
❏ Other: _____

Ask Yourself . . .

❖ Do you oppose or gladly receive the power of God?

❖ When you encounter worldly power and opposition to God, what is your response?

Write a prayer asking God for the power to discern the spirits of this world:

_____

_____

_____

Day 13

Experiencing God's Power

For the preaching of the cross is to them that perish foolishness; but unto us which are saved it is the power of God.

—1 CORINTHIANS 1:18

IN THE BIBLE *we read how men fell when they caught a glimpse of God's glory. Paul tells us there are those who have a form of godliness, but deny the power thereof; from such we are to turn away. "In the last days, perilous times shall come," and those who have reprobate minds shall withstand God's children to their faces, even as the magicians withstood Moses.*

In the last days, there will be some people living very near to God; but the devil will have his workers, too, who will attribute signs and wonders done to any power except the power of Christ. The Lamb of God, the Lion of the tribe of Judah, has never lost His power, and never will lose His power. I would hate to say, by my actions, that I thought the devil had more power than God.

There is a wonderful difference between the power of God and any of those other powers. The Holy Ghost comes only in Christ. He only comes into the bodies of those who love God. When He takes possession of us, He takes us away into the sweetest experience this side of heaven—that of being alone with God. He talks to us and reveals to us "things to come" (John 16).

The power of God changes us into the image of Christ, while the power of this world destroys us and brings destruction and death into our lives. Read

Galatians 2:20 and 2 Corinthians 3:18. On the cross below, write all the ways that the Spirit is conforming you to the image of Christ by His power:

_____
_____
_____
_____
_____
_____

$\mathcal{J}$T IS WONDERFUL! *God puts us under the power, and God takes us out. No man can bestow this power upon another. It comes only through Jesus Christ. There are two kinds of power, and people who do not know the difference will stand up today and say that wisdom is foolishness.*

The two kinds of power are God's power and the world's conterfeit power. God's power changes us and gives true life.

Read 2 Corinthians 5:17. Describe how the miracle-working power of God has changed your life and made you a new creation:

_____
_____
_____
_____

Ask Yourself . . .

❖ How are you being changed in Christ?
❖ What in you still needs to be changed by Christ?

Write a prayer asking Christ to conform you to His image by the power of His Spirit:

_____

_____

_____

Day 14

Signs of the Holy Ghost

And these signs shall follow them that believe.
—MARK 16:17

MANY PEOPLE TODAY *have an intellectual faith and a historical faith. They believe. Well, the devils believe and tremble. Belief is one thing, but faith is another. "The letter killeth; the Spirit giveth life." If the truth is hid, it is hid to those who are lost.*

We may have intellectual imaginations, go through a course of study, and learn the doctrines of men. However, no one but the Holy Ghost can give us knowledge of "the things of God." They seem foolishness to the natural man. Sometimes the Holy Ghost gives a spirit of laughter, and sometimes one of weeping, with everyone in the place being affected by the Spirit.

I have stood before thousands of people, and could not speak, just weep. When I was able to see, people were weeping everywhere. That is one way the Holy Ghost works. I have stood for an hour with my hand raised, held by the mighty power of God. When I came to myself and saw the people, their faces were shining.

When the power of the Holy Spirit comes upon you, how are you affected by His miracle-working power? Circle all that apply to you.

I am changed.   I am renewed and revived.
I weep with repentance.   I weep for joy.
I laugh.   I dance.
I shout.   I sing unto the Lord.

I worship and praise Him.
I fall down in His presence.
I shake and tremble in His presence.
Other: _____

OD MOVES IN *mysterious ways His wonders to perform. He is the God I worship. Jesus says, "Behold I and the children which God hath given me" (Heb. 2:13). We believe in signs and wonders, not from beneath but from above. We are a people to be wondered at. We are a sign among the people.*

Read Acts 4. Look for all the changes in the early believers wrought by the power of the Holy Spirit. List below the changes that you observe. Circle any changes that you personally need to make in your own spiritual life:

_____
_____
_____

Ask Yourself . . .

❖ What miraculous changes has Christ made in my life this past week?
❖ What changes does He still need to make?

Write a prayer asking the Holy Spirit to change you His way, to do His will, in His timing:

_____
_____

Day 15

Joshua, Jericho, and Faith

By faith the walls of Jericho fell down, after they were compassed about seven days.

—HEBREWS 11:30

RULY, GOD MOVES *in a mysterious way. Remember the fall of Jericho? Jericho had great walls around it, and all the people were shut in. God said to Joshua that he and his men of war should march around the city once a day for six days, with seven priests bearing before the ark seven trumpets of rams' horns. On the seventh day they were to march around the city seven times, with the priests blowing the trumpets. When they made a long trumpet blast the people were to shout, and the walls should fall down.*

Read Joshua 6. Look carefully at this miracle. As you read, think about the mountains or walls in your life that need to be taken down by the Lord. Write down the areas where God desires to pull down hindrances that are keeping you from achieving victory in your life.

_____

_____

_____

_____

_____

_____

_____

T TOOK FAITH *to do all that marching without any sign of victory; to shout—anyone can shout after the walls fall. Humanly speaking, how foolish this all was, don't you see? No preparation for war, only marching and blowing rams' horns, but that was God's way, and they were silly enough to obey God! What was the result? The walls went down.*

So we could go through all the Word of God. So many things that seem so silly. God asked His people to do things people would laugh at, but it was God's way, and His servants were willing to obey Him. The result showed God's wonderful wisdom and brought victory through a visible display of His power.

God's wisdom in facing your battles is God's best— God's way in God's time. Consider some of the problems or decisions you are facing. Choose one of those problems, and then complete these sentences:

The problem, battle, or decision I face is _____

_____ .

God's best in this situation is _____

_____ .

God's way to handle this is _____

_____ .

God's timing for winning this victory is _____

_____ .

Day 15

Ask Yourself . . .

❖ What battles are you trying to fight by your-self?

❖ What happens when you try to force your timing upon a problem?

Write a prayer seeking God's best, His way, and His timing for your problems:

_____

_____

_____

Day 16

The Deep Things of God

But God hath revealed them unto us by his Spirit: for the Spirit searcheth all things, yea, the deep things of God.

—1 Corinthians 2:10

THE SPIRIT OF God lets us down into the deep things, even the deep things of God. Peter fell into a trance upon the housetop, and God spoke to him three times. Paul and Silas started out to visit converts. Paul had a vision; he saw a man of Macedonia holding out his hands and saying, "Come over and help us." He knew it was the call of God, so they changed their course and went to a place altogether different than their plans.

When Paul and Silas began to preach and were arrested, they might have thought they had been mistaken about God's call. But Paul knew God, and he never doubted that it was God's voice that had called him. They might have said, "We would have had many people to preach to if we had not come here, but now we have been put in prison with our feet fast in the stocks." The devil put them in there, but God permitted it, and God delivered them.

When you find yourself in the midst of a difficult trial or test, how do you respond? God tests us. Satan tempts us. Our faith is refined in fire like fine gold. We can either become better or bitter. Check the feelings you have when your faith is being refined:

❑ Thankful and filled with praise
❑ Upset and worried
❑ Cautious and careful
❑ Determined to stay the course and stand firm
❑ Complaining and resentful
❑ Other: _____

Part of the miracle we need when we find ourselves facing difficulties is the inner strength and grace to persevere. Read Romans 5:1–5, and on the blocks below, write the name of each block of hope recorded in the verses that you read:

Now complete these sentences:

From past tribulations I have learned that God _____
_____.

I have learned to be patient when _____
_____.

The part of my character that was strengthened by patiently enduring trials was _____
_____.

Now when I face trials, my hope is _____

_____ .

THERE ARE MANY *wonderful things for us in these last days—demonstrations of God's power that the natural man cannot understand. There are other powers too, and many do not know the difference. God's power is the greatest, and is the only power that will bring peace to your soul.*

A wonderful demonstration of God's power in our lives is the inner peace He gives when we go through tough places. We learn that tough times never last but tough people strengthened by His grace not only last, but overcome.

Read Romans 8:35–39 and Philippians 4:6–7, 12–13. Rewrite these passages in your own words, expressing how God gives you inner peace and victory in every circumstance. _____

Ask Yourself . . .

❖ Do you view miracles as a way to escape difficulties, or as the means to persevere in spite of trials?

❖ Do you rejoice in the midst of all trials?

Write a prayer asking God to give you the miracle of inner peace when facing outer turmoil:

Day 17

God's Glory

*Now when Solomon had made an end of praying, the
fire came down from heaven, and consumed the burnt
offering . . . and the glory of the Lord filled the house.*
                                    —2 CHRONICLES 7:1

IT [THE GLORY OF THE LORD] *represented Pentecost: "When
Solomon had made an end of praying." So many people expect
God to answer. They would be frightened if He did. Solomon
stretched out his hands and prayed to God, and God heard him.*

*When he had made an end of praying, something happened. God
will come forth if you are not afraid of the power, if you are ready to stand
for God with all there is of you. As Pentecostal people we should always
be "prayed up," so we can get hold of God quickly, and be sure it is for
the glory of God.*

How do you get prepared and prayed up so that you
are ready for God's glory in your life? Check all that
apply:

❑ I worship and praise God.
❑ I pray in the Spirit and intercede.
❑ I spend time reading God's Word and praying.
❑ I crucify my flesh and repent daily.
❑ Other: _____

HE FIRE CAME DOWN *from heaven, and consumed the burnt offering and the sacrifices; and the glory of the Lord filled the house" (v. 1). Some people talk as if God never had any glory, as though the glory of God was never seen at any time.*

Paul said, *"For if the ministration of condemnation be glory, much more doth the ministration of righteousness exceed in glory"* (2 Cor. 3:9).

The glory under the law did not last; but the Holy Ghost came at Pentecost to stay. And the manifestations under the ministry of the Holy Ghost are to be with much greater glory, to "exceed in glory." The power under the law was only a shadow of what we ought to have under grace. This was the ministry of life, not death.

By His Spirit, Christ is transforming us from glory to glory (2 Cor. 3:18). What is the purpose of this transformation? Read the following verses, and write down how Christ is transforming your life:

Colossians 1:9–14 _____

Ephesians 1:7–1 _____

Galatians 5:2–26 _____

Romans 8:1–3 _____

Day 17

In changing us from glory to glory, Christ does not change us because we earn it, but because of His mercy and grace. Our part is to continue in obedience and surrender to Him.

Ask Yourself . . .

❖ How are you preparing yourself to receive His glory?

❖ What new thing is Christ doing in your life today?

Write a prayer praising God for His glory, manifested in Christ Jesus.

_____

_____

_____

Day 18

God's Power Shines Forth

*Go and show John again those things which ye do
hear and see.*

—Matthew 11:4

---

*W*HAT A WONDERFUL *people we are in our privileges! Today
everyone may be God's priest. If we abide in Him and His
words abide in us, we may ask what we will and it shall be
done. We indeed have wonderful privileges. The power of the Lord
shines forth a hundred times greater than under the law.*

*When John was in prison he began to doubt whether Jesus was the
Christ, and he sent his disciples to ask, "Art Thou He that should
come?" Jesus did not say, "I belong to the church or I belong to a college." He told John's disciples to tell John the things they have seen—
the lame walked, the blind could see, different diseases were healed,
and the poor had the gospel preached to them. "Blessed is he, whoso-
ever shall not be offended" (Matt. 11:6). Men get mad at the signs of
the Holy Ghost. They become jealous, spitting out hatred and trying
to tear down God's work.*

Miracles are signs that point to God's acting in history.
If a miracle points to a man or institution, then it is
counterfeit. When unbelievers encounter God's miracles,
they are either awed by His power or angry. Why?
Because men are always humbled when God acts. So
prideful human intellect always hates God's miracles.
Read Mark 7:1–23. On the next page, summarize Jesus'
description of the heart that is against God's ways:

_____

_____

_____

F JOHN DID *not believe in Christ through the signs, no eloquence would be of value. If he did not believe what the witnesses told him he would not believe anything.*

Neither will you! If you only look on, it will seem foolishness to you as we praise God, get filled with the Holy Ghost, and get gifts. But it is Jesus first, last, and all the time. We hold up Jesus and praise His name. We see bright, happy faces. We see pain go out of bodies, and we go home rejoicing.

A well-known phrase asserted, *Expect a miracle!* Jesus seems to have put a slightly differently slant on this perspective. When you *Expect Jesus!* then miracles happen. So go beyond expecting miracles to expecting the God of all miracles to act in love and grace. When you witness a miracle from God, how do you repond? Circle all your responses or feelings:

Joy	Pride	Anger
Hope	Praise	Frustration
Awe	Wonder	Amazement
Doubt		

Opposing God's miracles today denies that He is the same yesterday, today, and tomorrow (Heb. 13:8).

Ask Yourself . . .

❖ Are your eyes and ears open to the miracles of God?

❖ Will you ask God to make you aware of His miracles all around you?

Write a prayer praising God for doing miracles today:

_____

_____

_____

Day 19

Suddenly

*And suddenly there came a sound from heaven as of a
rushing mighty wind, and it filled all the house.*

—ACTS 2:2

AT PENTECOST, suddenly they heard a sound like a mighty,
rushing wind. This Holy Ghost we are holding up is a mighty
power. He came suddenly from heaven, like a windstorm, like
floods of water filling the vessels, and as fire upon the heads of one
hundred twenty people.

As it were, cloven tongues of fire sat upon their heads. Then the
Holy Ghost went in and took possession of the temple. He took full
possession of the machinery, wound it up, and set it running for God.
They staggered like drunken people and fell. This mighty power took
possession of their tongues, and spoke through them in other
languages.

Away back in the times of the prophets, God said that through
men of "stammering lips and another tongue will He speak to this
people." Think of that! God's doing such a mighty thing! But some do
not want to believe. That is the way the Holy Ghost came, and still
comes today; and people say it is some other power.

If you had been alive and with those first disciples at
Pentecost and spoke in tongues as they did, how would
you have responded? Put an *x* on the line to indicate your
response:

Excited	Afraid

Bold	Timid

Filled with faith	Doubtful

Hungering for more	Uncertain

The same power that the disciples experienced during Pentecost is available to you. Are you willing to receive? Or do your human reasoning and doubts keep you at arm's length from receiving all God has for you?

HEY DID NOT lose their minds; they had just found them! They had the spirit of love and of a sound mind. We never have a sound mind until we get the mind of Christ. People who cannot understand say these things are foolishness. We are told the wisdom of this world is foolishness with God. This is the power and wisdom of God, not the work of the devil; people saying so doesn't make it so.

God had complete control. Suddenly, He came in and took possession. The Holy Ghost is in the world today.

When God took complete control of Samson's life (Judg. 13:8–16:31), Samson had miraculous power and strength. When the Spirit came upon him suddenly, he could defeat entire armies of men or pull down the gates of a city. But when Samson took back control of his life, no miracles would happen.

What do you need to surrender in order for God's Spirit to take complete control of your life? In the pie chart below, write down what you need to surrender now to the Spirit of God:

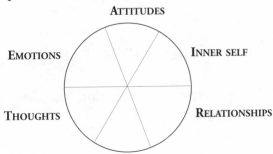

ATTITUDES

EMOTIONS

INNER SELF

THOUGHTS

RELATIONSHIPS

Ask Yourself . . .

❖ How would you react if the Spirit suddenly took control of your life as He did the disciples' lives at Pentecost?

❖ Is every area of your life ready for His complete control?

Write a prayer inviting the Holy Spirit to be in complete control of your life at all times and in all ways:

_____

_____

_____

Day 20

The Ministry of the Holy Spirit

But the manifestation of the Spirit is given to every man to profit.

—1 CORINTHIANS 12:7

THE PROFESSIONAL MINISTRY *does not want the gifts today. Christians are baptized with the Holy Ghost so that the whole body may be edified.*

The working of the Holy Ghost is the visible sign of the presence of Jesus. They went from Jerusalem to preach the gospel, and the Lord was with them. I love that word. He is in heaven — but He is also with us.

The Lord was with them, confirming the Word. How? With signs and wonders following. Wherever they went they saw faces shine, someone healed, someone speaking in tongues. This you see and hear — it is the Holy Ghost — and it is for the work of the ministry. We do not need professional ministers. Everyone filled with the Holy Ghost can minister in the gifts.

What signs and wonders are following your life? With what gifts are you ministering? Read 1 Corinthians 12:1–11, and list the nine gifts mentioned there. Then circle the gifts that are operating in your life, and underline those that you would pray for the Spirit to manifest through you:

1. _____

2. _____

3. _____

4. _____

5. _____

6. _____

7. _____

8. _____

9. _____

HAVE TESTED THE *truth; I know it is of God. How can we help talking of the things we have seen? I have seen things by the Spirit, and in visions. I have seen Jesus, the heavens open, the marriage supper, hosts of angels, the glory of God. I have seen them, glory to God! I know what I am telling you. I know Jesus lives and is standing by my side more truly than I know you are here. These things are verities.*

I am not ashamed of the gospel of Christ. Glory to God! When a weak woman comes here to tell you what strong men in the ministry ought to have told you, what are you going to think about it? I say these things are true; and when people say they are foolishness and fanaticism, dare they attempt to prove it by the Word? I dare them to do it.

A great miracle that the Spirit works in the life of the believer is a supernatural boldness for witnessing. Are you bold for Christ or simply lukewarm? Rate where you are right now. Circle the number that best represents your relationship with Christ from 1 *(cold)*, to 5 *(hot)*:

My love for Christ.

| 1 | 2 | 3 | 4 | 5 |

My boldness in witnessing to others.

| 1 | 2 | 3 | 4 | 5 |

My hunger for His presence.

| 1 | 2 | 3 | 4 | 5 |

My zeal to know Him more and more.

| 1 | 2 | 3 | 4 | 5 |

My desire to fellowship with His sufferings.

| 1 | 2 | 3 | 4 | 5 |

My commitment to serve Him.

| 1 | 2 | 3 | 4 | 5 |

Ask Yourself . . .

❖ Is there any situation in which you are ashamed of Christ?

❖ Where in your life does your passion for Christ need to grow hotter?

Write a prayer asking Christ to intensify your passion for Him:

_____

_____

_____

Day 21

The Spirit's Outpouring

And it shall come to pass in the last days, saith God,
I will pour out of my Spirit upon all flesh . . . And I
will show wonders in heaven above.

—ACTS 2:17, 19

HIS IS A *wonderful scripture, and many do not understand it.*
There is a certain time spoken of here, when certain great and
wonderful things shall take place and people shall know that
prophecy is being fulfilled. "It shall come to pass in the last days, I will
pour out My Spirit," and there shall be signs in the heavens and the
earth—signs of His coming.

This prophecy was first spoken eight hundred years before Jesus
came to earth. Peter, standing up on the day of Pentecost, confirmed
it. Under the inspiration of the Holy Ghost, on fire with the Holy
Ghost from head to foot, he said these things would come to pass in
the last days.

Three miracles of the Spirit's outpouring are prophecy, dreams, and visions. Read Acts 2:17–21, and then answer these questions:

When the Spirit outpours, who prophesies? _____

_____

Who receives dreams and visions? _____

_____

What miracle is seen with the outpouring? _____

_____

W E BELIEVE AND *know by the Word of God, and by the signs, that we are now living in the last days, the very times Peter spoke about when we were to know by the mighty things taking place. We are the people, and this is the time just before the "notable day of the Lord" bursts upon the world. We believe we are the people, yea we know it.*

How have you experienced the outpouring of the Holy Spirit in your life? Complete these sentences:

One dream the Spirit has given me is _____

_____.

One vision the Spirit has given me is _____

_____.

One prophecy the Spirit has given me is _____

_____.

A person I have led to Christ is _____

_____.

Ask Yourself . . .

❖ How are you encountering the outpouring of His Spirit?

❖ To whom are you witnessing right now about accepting Christ?

Write a prayer asking God's Spirit to inspire His prophecy, dreams, and visions in you:

_____

_____

_____

Day 22

Ready for the Flood

I will pour out of my Spirit upon all flesh.

—ACTS 2:17

NOT SPRINKLE A *few drops, but pour out on all flesh—a cloudburst! Just at the end, it will continue until the saints are taken away then the tribulation will burst upon the earth. The sign will be that your sons and daughters, not everybody's—your sons and daughters—shall prophesy. It is very plain so that everyone may understand.*

Have you ever experienced prophecy? To prophesy is to speak forth God's Word to others. How does the Spirit speak the Word to you? Check all the ways you have encountered prophecy:

- ❏ Through sermons
- ❏ Through Bible teaching
- ❏ Through someone speaking prophetically
- ❏ Through tongues and interpretation
- ❏ Through visions and dreams
- ❏ Through prayer
- ❏ Through reading, studying, and praying Scripture
- ❏ Other: _____

When you hear God's Word, how should you respond? Jesus answers this question with His parable of the sower and his seed. Read Mark 4:1–20. Complete these sentences:

The soil of my heart is most like the soil that _____

_____.

When I hear God's Word, I usually _____

_____.

When I obey His Word, God _____

_____.

Y̶OUR SONS AND *your daughters will prophesy." There is to be a wonderful ministry in the last days. Paul says male and female are one in Christ. Both shall prophesy in the last days.*
That is the effect of the outpouring of the Holy Ghost. And there are other signs:

❖ *Devils shall be cast out.*
❖ *Hands shall be laid on the sick, and they shall recover.*
❖ *If anyone drinks poison accidentally, it shall not hurt him.*
❖ *Many shall speak with new tongues.*
❖ *Serpents shall not be able to hurt believers in the last days.*

Are you under the cloudburst? Are you ready for the Spirit's flood?

Read Mark 16:15–18 aloud. Replace each "they" with the pronoun "I." Then answer *true* or *false* to each statement below: (Mark *T* for true in your life, and *F* for false.)

_____ 1. I have prayed for people and they have been delivered from evil and demons.

_____ 2. I lay hands on and pray for the sick.

_____ 3. Whenever evil attacks me, I am not hurt.

_____ 4. I speak in new tongues.

Ask Yourself . . .

- ❖ Are signs and wonders following you?
- ❖ Are you hindering the power of the Spirit from working in your life?
- ❖ Are you listening to the prophetic voice of the Spirit speaking to your heart?

Write a prayer asking Jesus to prepare the soil of your heart to receive whatever prophetic word He has for you:

_____

_____

_____

Day 23

To See God's Throne

And they chose Stephen, a man full of faith and of the Holy Ghost.

—ACTS 6:5

REMEMBER THE FIRST *martyr, Stephen? He was a man full of faith, wisdom, and power. He was full of the Holy Ghost. The wise men tried to confound him, but could not do it; then they were jealous and wanted to get rid of him. They hired men of the baser sort who lied about this mighty servant of God.*

They arrested him, and there he was before the great assembly. He did not try to defend himself, but he took the opportunity offered to preach to them about Jesus. He was filled with the Holy Ghost. His face was like the face of an angel, and those who swore his life away saw it. He did not look like a liar and a hypocrite. He was a servant of almighty God.

Read Acts 6–7, and then complete the following sentences:

One way my faith is like Stephen's is _____

_____.

One way I am not like Stephen is _____

_____.

If I faced dying for Christ, I would _____

_____ .

To die for Jesus would be _____

_____ .

SOMETIMES YOU CAN *see that light today in the faces of God's children. Stephen looked up into heaven and saw the glory of God. He saw Jesus who had risen from the dead, standing at the right hand of God, and he told the people, "Oh, Lord, open the eyes of these people, and let them see the angels of the Lord encamped around about us and Jesus standing in the midst!" When Stephen told what he saw, the evil men gnashed their teeth. They did not intend to repent. They dragged him out and stoned him to death, but the Lord received him and permitted it. God promises His people shall be protected, and it is no sign that He forsakes them because trouble comes. Stephen's enemies did not like it because God received him, nor did they like to see his face shine with the glory of God. His body was lying a bruised mass, but he rose to meet the Lord. He had a glorious vision.*

What words best describe Stephen's miraculous faith? Circle all the words you believe best describe His wonder-working faith:

Bold	Courageous	Assured
Dynamic	Unafraid	Sharp
Sharp	Convicting	Real
Other: _____		

Ask Yourself . . .

- ❖ What needs to happen in your life for your faith to be like Stephen's?
- ❖ What miracles might happen in your life if you were more like Stephen?

Read Hebrews 11, and then write a prayer thanking God for heroes of the faith like Stephen and the others mentioned in that chapter:

_____

_____

_____

Day 24

Not I, but Christ

Then Peter said, Silver and gold have I none, but,
such as I have give I thee: In the name of Jesus Christ
of Nazareth rise up and walk.

—ACTS 3:6

IN THE NEW *Testament, signs and wonders were done before the*
people. Wherever Jesus went, the people followed Him. God was
with Him, putting fear upon the people through miracles, signs,
and wonders that God wrought through Him.

He said, "I speak not of myself: but the Father that dwelleth in me,
he doeth the works" (John 14:10). When the rulers, elders, and scribes
demanded to know from Peter: "By what power, or by what name,
have ye done this [healed the impotent man]?," Peter responded: "Be
it known unto you all, and to all the people of Israel, that by the name
of Jesus Christ of Nazareth, whom ye crucified, whom God raised
from the dead, even by him doth this man stand here before you
whole" (Acts 4:7, 10). Not I, but Christ. It is the same today.

We do not heal; Christ heals. We do not work miracles; Christ is the miracle-worker. Never touch His glory.
In Him all things are possible. Apart from Christ,
nothing is possible.

Take a moment. Make a list of all the miracles that
have happened in your life over the last week. Then
stand; lift your hands; and with a shout or a song give
Christ glory.

Miracles

I N THE SIGNS *and wonders today, it is "Not I, but Christ." He dwells in these bodies, and the work is done by the mighty power of the Holy Ghost. "Know ye not that your body is the temple of the Holy Ghost?" Jesus Christ dwells in us. We are God's powerhouse.*

How does Christ perform miracles today? *Through us.* We are His tabernacles and His dwelling place. Read the following verses, and write down how Christ indwells us:

John 6:51–57 _____

1 Corinthians 3:16 _____

1 Corinthians 6:19–20 _____

Colossians 1:27 _____

Ask Yourself . . .

❖ Is Christ indwelling you and working His miracles through you?

❖ How are you glorifying Him daily with your worship and praise?

Write a prayer thanking Christ for His indwelling in your life:

_____

_____

_____

Day 25

Press the Battle to the Gates

Nay, in all these things we are more than conquerors through him that loved us.

—ROMANS 8:37

IT WAS BY THE *hands of the apostles, not of angels, that God did His mighty works; and people believed when the signs followed.*

Jesus commanded the unclean spirits to come out, and they had to come; the power of the Holy Spirit went through the apostles' hands. That is just the way God works today.

The apostles were not afraid of persecution, the sword, or anything else. They were willing to face death in any form rather than disgrace the cause of Christ by being cowards. It is a mighty God we serve, and today, Jesus Christ who ascended into heaven is here by my side. He will lead His hosts on to victory. Let us press the battle to the gates.

Miracles do not stop men from persecuting God's saints. Jesus performed miracles and was persecuted. After Pentecost, God worked miracles at the hands of the apostles, and they were persecuted. Such has been the case throughout church history. If you desire to see God's miracle-working power in your life, expect persecution. Read the following passages, and write down how we are to respond to persecution:

Matthew 5:10–12

Luke 6:22–23

John 16:32–33

Acts 4:1–31

1 Peter 1:1–9

HIS SECT [PENTECOSTAL] *is always spoken against, mis-represented, and lied about; but Jesus Christ is leading on His hosts. God permitted Jesus to be nailed to the cross and laid in the grave, but He came forth like the sun.*

God permitted the apostles to be arrested and put in prison; then He had an opportunity to show His power. He sent His angel and delivered them. The angel of the Lord is with His own. Our citizenship is in heaven. We are children of the King.

Around us day and night are ministering spirits sent to minister to those who are heirs of salvation. We can afford to be misrepresented or even put in prison if only we are looking for the manifestation and the glory of translation that will sweep us through the gates.

When God does something miraculous in your life and others are doubtful or critical of you, how do you respond? Prioritize your responses from the *first step* (1) you would take, to the *last step* (5).

_____ I pray.

_____ I praise God and thank Him for His protection.

_____ I rejoice that I can suffer for Christ.

_____ I reach out for fellowship, support, prayer, and sharing with other Christians.

_____ I put on the armor of God and resist the enemy.

_____ Other

Ask Yourself . . .

❖ Are you prepared for the battle when God's miracles, signs, and wonders are unleashed around you?

❖ Do you desire all that God has for you by His Spirit?

Write a prayer thanking Him for seeing you through every battle and valley:

_____

_____

_____

Day 26

Do Not Stifle God's Spirit

Quench not the Spirit.

—1 Thessalonians 5:19

H̲E WILL NOT *only come in healing power, but will manifest Himself in many mighty ways. On the day of Pentecost, Peter said, "God hath poured forth this which ye see and hear." And from what they heard and saw, three thousand knew it was the power of God and turned to Christ. Others stifled conviction and turned away saying, "This is the work of the devil."*

When the Holy Ghost is poured out, it is either life unto life or death unto death. It is life unto life to those who go forward, and death unto death to those who blaspheme against the Holy Ghost. So we want to be careful what we say against the divers operations, supernatural signs, and workings of the Holy Ghost. Some people look on and say, "It looks like hypnotism," or, "I believe it is mesmerism."

To others it appears mere foolishness, even as Scripture says of the natural man, "The natural man receiveth not the things of the Spirit of God: for they are foolishness unto him: neither can he know them, because they are spiritually discerned" (1 Cor. 2:14). Have you received of the life of the Spirit, or are you stifling His conviction?

What God does miraculously can never be discerned in the natural. Only what is spiritual can discern what is of the Spirit. On each line below, write what that verse says about human wisdom or the revelation of God's wisdom.

1 Corinthians 1:27

1 Corinthians 1:30

1 Corinthians 2:4

1 Corinthians 2:5–6

1 Corinthians 2:13

1 Corinthians 2:14

1 Corinthians 2:16

Ask Yourself . . .

❖ Are you discerning the spiritual things in your life?
❖ Are you listening to the voice of the Holy Spirit?

Write a prayer asking God to give you the mind of Christ:

Day 27

God's Power Cannot Be Bought

But Peter said unto him, Thy money perish with thee, because thou hast thought that the gift of God may be purchased with money.

—ACTS 8:20

REACH IN A *simple way, and demonstrate. The seal is put upon the Word by the Holy Spirit. Many say that when we lay hands upon the people they get mesmerized. I am sorry they do not know more of the power of God. There was a great revival at Samaria. Simon the sorcerer was baptized, but none of them had been baptized with the Holy Ghost. Peter and John went to Samaria and laid hands on them, and they received the Holy Ghost.*

Simon recognized the power was different from sorcery, and he wanted it. He offered them money to give him this power, that whomsoever he laid hands on might receive the Holy Ghost. The apostles were horrified. They said, "Thy money perish with thee, because thou hast thought that the gift of God can be purchased with money" (Acts 8:20).

God cannot be bought. We cannot manipulate God to act miraculously in our lives. We always yield ourselves to His will, His way, and His timing.

When you give to the Lord, how do you feel, and what is your attitude? Circle all the attitudes and feelings you have when you give:

Expect something in return   Joyful
Grateful to God   Seeking future reward
Loving God   Desiring to please God
Other: _____

Simon had the wrong motivation for giving. Read the following verses, and write down what the Bible says about giving:

Matthew 6:19–24 _____

_____

Mark 12:41–44 _____

_____

Luke 6:38 _____

_____

2 Corinthians 8:7–9 _____

_____

2 Corinthians 9:6–7 _____

_____

HE HOLY GHOST *and His power are gifts of God. No one can buy them. Many people today do not understand any more than Simon did.*

By the laying on of the apostles' hands something happened: the Holy Ghost fell on those people, and they had great blessing.

The gifts of the Spirit are acts of grace given by the Holy Spirit. They cannot be earned, bought, manipulated, or controlled. God's miraculous power working in us depends on our being yielded totally and completely to Him. Are you yielded? Below is a circle which represents your life. The inner circle is your spirit. The next is your soul. And the outer circle is your physical being. (See 1 Thessalonians 5:23.) Shade each circle to the level that part of your life is yielded to the Spirit's control:

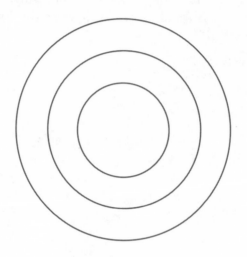

Ask Yourself . . .

❖ What parts of your life still need to be totally yielded to the Lord?
❖ Are you willing to have everything in your life under His complete control?

Write a prayer asking the Holy Spirit to sanctify every part of your life:

_____

_____

_____

Day 28

The Power of His Resurrection

*Behold, I show you a mystery; We shall not all sleep,
but we shall all be changed, in a moment, in the
twinkling of an eye, at the last trump.*
— 1 CORINTHIANS 15:51–52

NOTHING BUT THE *mighty Holy Ghost will ever take you up in the clouds. He will quicken these mortal bodies, and they will be changed. We shall not have wings, but our hands and feet will be made light. Our feet shall be like "hind's feet" and we will run, skip, and almost fly. We shall know the power of the resurrection life. We shall be so filled with the Holy Ghost that our bodies will be made light. Sometimes my body is made so light, I can hardly stay.*

My feet are on the earth, but my hands seem on the throne. Christ arose from the dead, and He is the resurrection and the life. People want to get the blood of Jesus over them, over their diseased bodies, in His name.

Do you believe right now? If you believe and praise the Lord in faith it shall be done. If you do not feel the joy, offer praise as a sacrifice, and ask God to give you the joy. When the unclean spirit is driven out, the disease goes, and the resurrection life comes into you.

Some of the greatest miracles you will ever witness will be the miracles that God does in your life. And the greatest miracles are yet to come. What miracles from the Lord are you praying for in the near future? What ones in the distant future? Describe three of them:

1.

2.

3.

ℭOME DANCE, SHOUT, *and praise the Lord as the life of Jesus thrills through them. I declare to you on the authority of God and from my own experience, I know it is the power of God through Jesus Christ. It does not take Jesus long to do the work, but it takes some of us a long time to get there. Five minutes will do the work. Then the peace of God will flow through you like a river, and you will have joy in the Holy Ghost. As you go home, do not think about your sins. Don't commit any more sins, and don't worry about the past because it is under the blood.*

Begin to praise God for what He is and what He will do in your life. Set aside the past, and praise Him for His goodness and faithfulness. Complete these sentences:

I praise God because in the past He

.

I praise God because now He

.

I praise God because in the future He will

.

Ask Yourself . . .

- ❖ What miraculous thing is God doing right now in your life?
- ❖ Is your life filled with praise or with requests?

Write a prayer of praise to the miracle-working God:

Day 29

Pentecostal Revival

And by the hands of the apostles were many signs and wonders wrought among the people; and they were all with one accord in Solomon's porch.

—ACTS 5:12

THIS WAS THE *greatest revival given in the New Testament—greater in many ways than Pentecost. Then they were all with one accord and in place while awaiting the outpouring of the Spirit. You get there, and God will shake the country.*

Signs and wonders were wrought and of the rest dare no man join himself unto them. They were so full of fire no person dared say falsely, "I am one of you." They were afraid God would strike them dead.

God wants to get a people so full of His power that others full of wildfire will say, "God, fill me with the real power."

What brings revival? Read again Acts 1–2, and then list all those things that brought revival to the disciples:

_____

_____

Your list included things like prayer, unity among the believers, patiently waiting upon God, repentance, and a hunger for God's Spirit in power.

Describe what God needs to do in your life in order to bring revival to you, enabling His signs and wonders to be manifested in your life.

_____

_____

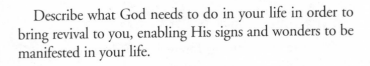

W HAT WAS THE *result of Pentecost? Believers were added to the church? No, they were added to the Lord, both men and women. Some say that this excitement and fanaticism is good enough for women, but there was also a multitude of strong-minded men there.*

They brought the sick into the streets and laid them on beds and couches so that Peter's shadow might overshadow some of them. See what a cranky set they were! I wish we were just like that. Excitement rose higher and higher. The whole country was stirred. There came multitudes from the city of Jerusalem, bringing the sick, and they were healed. Why? Because they came seeking God and not man. A wonderful revival, was it not?

Read 2 Chronicles 7:14 and Acts 3:19. Describe how revival comes to God's people through prayer:

_____

_____

Revival begins with prayer and repentance. Revival is manifested when the power of the Holy Spirit is poured out from heaven. Such revival overflows with miracles—lives being saved, delivered, healed, and set free in the name of Jesus.

Ask Yourself . . .

❖ Are you praying for revival in your own life and in your church?

❖ Where do you see the evidences of revival?

Write a prayer asking God to pour out His Spirit in revival as He did at Pentecost:

_____

_____

_____

Day 30

Healing and Praise

And immediately he [the paralytic] arose, took up the bed, and went forth before them all; insomuch that they were all amazed, and glorified God.

—MARK 2:12

THE PARALYTIC DID *not break up the meeting when he was brought to Jesus and dropped down through the roof while Jesus was preaching. Jesus is our example. He was glad to have something like that happen, because it gave Him a chance to show His power. Jesus forgave the man all his sins and then made him rise, take up his bed, and walk.*

The people began to shout, "Glory," the same way you do here. You cannot help it. If you have not done it you will. A consumptive woman was brought in here in her night robe. I did not care what she had on—she was healed. Hallelujah!

When the paralytic was healed, they gave glory to God. People say today, "You never heard such a noisy group." If they had only heard them then! We have something to make a fuss about. Dead people never make much noise, do they? There is not much noise in a graveyard!

What miracles are you giving God praise for right now? Complete the following statements of praise:

Jesus, I praise You for saving me from _____

_____.

Jesus, I praise You for healing me from _____

_____ .

Jesus, I praise You for delivering me from _____

_____ .

Jesus, I praise You for setting me free from _____

_____ .

Take a moment to reflect on what you have learned and discovered about God's miracle-working power from this study. Then complete these sentences:

A miracle is when God _____

_____ .

The miracles I see God doing every day are _____

_____ .

A miracle God has recently performed in my life is _____

_____ .

One hindrance to miracles in my life is _____

_____ .

I am praying for a miracle _____

_____ .

Expect more than a miracle. Expect Jesus to pour out and baptize you with His Holy Spirit. When you have His presence in your life, your life is lived within the miracle-potent atmosphere of the Holy Spirit.

Ask Yourself . . .

❖ Are you praising God every day for His miracles?

❖ Are you seeking the power of the Holy Spirit daily in your life?

Write a prayer praising God for the miracle of salvation and eternal life through His Son Jesus Christ:

_____

_____

_____

Leader's Guide

For Group Sessions

This devotional study is an excellent resource for group study including such settings as:

- ❖ Sunday school classes and other church classes.
- ❖ Prayer groups.
- ❖ Bible study groups.
- ❖ Ministries involving small groups, home groups, and accountability groups.
- ❖ Study groups for youth and adults.

Before the first session

- ❖ Contact everyone interested or already participating in the group about the meeting time, date, and place.
- ❖ Make certain that everyone has a copy of this devotional study guide, *The Original Maria Woodworth-Etter Devotional*, and the *Holy Spirit Encounter Bible.*
- ❖ Ask group members to begin their daily encounters in this guide. Plan for six sessions with each group session covering five devotional studies. Group members who faithfully do a devotional each day will be prepared to share in the group sessions. Plan out all your sessions before starting the first session.
- ❖ Pray for the Holy Spirit to guide, teach, and help each participant.
- ❖ Be certain that the place where you will meet has a chalkboard, white board, or flip chart with

appropriate writing materials. It is also best to be in a setting with movable, not fixed, seating.

Planning the Group Sessions

1. You will have six sessions together as a group. Plan to cover at least five days in each session.

2. In your first session, allow group members to select a partner with whom they will share and pray during each session. Keep the same pairs throughout the group sessions. You can put pairs together randomly—men with men and women with women.

3. Begin each session with prayer.

4. Read or ask group members to read the key scriptures at the start of each daily devotional for the five days prior to that session.

5. Prior to each session, decide which exercises and questions you would like to cover from the five daily devotional studies for that session.

6. Decide which exercises and sessions will be most appropriate for your group to share as a whole and which would be more comfortable for group members to share in pairs.

7. From the five previous days, decide which prayer(s) you wish the pairs to pray with one another.

8. Close each session with each group member sharing with the total group how he or she grew in faith during the previous week. Then lead the group in prayer or have group members pray aloud. Close the session with your own prayer.

9. In the last session, use the thirtieth day as an in-depth sharing time in pairs. Invite all the

group members to share the most important thing they learned about miracles during this study, and how their relationship with the Lord was deepened during the study. Close with prayers of praise and thanksgiving.

10. Whether sharing in pairs or as a total group, remember to allow each person the freedom not to share if they are not comfortable.

11. Be careful. This is not a therapy group. Group members who seek to dominate group discussions with their own problems or questions should be ministered to by the group leader or pastor in a one-on-one setting outside of the group session.

12. Always start and end the group session on time, and seek to keep the session within a ninety-minute time frame.